THE STRUGGLE IS REAL
BUT SO IS GOD
Volume 2

ANDREW F CARTER

SHIFTED PRESS

This Devotional is dedicated to my friends, family, supporters and followers. The ones who have encouraged, motivated, inspired and believed in me. I am humbled and honored to be a vessel for the Holy Spirit and to be walking the path that God has planned for me. I give thanks, praise, honor and glory to my Lord and Savior, Jesus Christ.

"And whatever you do, in word or deed, do everything in the name of the Lord Jesus, giving thanks to God the Father through him."

Colossians 3:17

Introduction

Building anything worthwhile takes time, patience and consistency. Creating a stronger relationship with God requires the same. This devotional is designed to plunge you into the word of God, provoke thought with shared experiences, and to encourage insightful and meaningful prayer. The foundation of this devotional is to make time to engage with God. Over the next 31 days, take your time as you journey deeper into your understanding of who God is and who He says you are. I pray that the Holy Spirit will lead you, guide you and direct you with each days devotion. Regardless of what you're going through, always remember that the struggle is real, but so is God.

How To Use This Devotional

Each day is broken down into four sections outlined as a quick bible study for you. First section is led with scripture. Second section are my personal thoughts and commentary on that scripture. Third section is an intimate prayer between you and God. Fourth section is your personal application to write down what the scripture meant to you and how you can apply it to your day. My best recommendation is to read this daily devotional at your own pace. Take time to process the material and allow God to speak to you through it. I pray that the Holy Spirit would guide you and direct you; that He would give you eyes to see, ears to hear and a heart to understand the things God wants to show you. Be blessed my friends and take this time to really draw near to our creator, the closer you get to Him, the clearer His voice becomes.

DAY ONE

"For the Spirit God gave us does not make us timid, but gives us power, love and self-discipline."

2 Timothy 1:7

The word of God gives us power, strength, authority, boldness and confidence. We should never boast in ourselves because without God we are nothing. But in Him and through the Spirit we are more than conquerors. We have to stop letting the enemy and the world tell us we are weak, we should worry, we should be fearful, or any other lies they spew at us. Today is a new day! Equip yourself with the armor of God, pick up your cross and prepare yourself for the battle. You, yes you, are a warrior, not a worrier. Stand firm on the word of God and let's start acting like we know how this story ends.

PRAYER

Father God help me walk in the strength and authority given to me through the blood of Jesus. My trust is in Your word, my identity is in Christ and I know my worth as one of Your children. Thank You for always being present and my source of strength, in Jesus name I pray, amen.

NOTES

_____

_____

_____

_____

<u>MEANING</u>

What does today's scripture mean to you?

_____

_____

_____

_____

_____

_____

_____

_____

APPLICATION

How can you apply this to your day?

_____

_____

_____

_____

_____

_____

_____

_____

_____

DAY TWO

"Jesus Christ is the same yesterday and today and forever."

Hebrews 13:8

The world is changing all around us. People come and go. Material items rot and decay. Everything is in a constant state of change. That's life. Once I fully understood this, I choose to invest my time, energy and thoughts in the one who was, is and will forever be the same and that's Jesus. I choose to focus my attention on the things of God. That's where I put all my trust. That's where my faith lies. My hope is in Him. I'm building my life on the foundation of the unmovable, unshakeable and unchanging God of Heaven, Earth and all creation. Knowing He never changes reassures me that we have a good father.

PRAYER

Lord I turn my eyes to Heaven and seek only the things of the spirit. Help me to stay focused on Your plan, purpose and will. If it's not from You, I pray that You strike it down and make my path clear. In Jesus name I pray, amen.

NOTES

_____

_____

_____

_____

MEANING

What does today's scripture mean to you?

_____

_____

_____

_____

_____

_____

_____

_____

_____

<u>APPLICATION</u>

How can you apply this to your day?

_____

_____

_____

_____

_____

_____

_____

_____

DAY THREE

"Now faith is confidence in what we hope for and assurance about what we do not see."
Hebrews 11:1

God is faithful. He always comes through. His love, mercy and grace exceed my expectation and comprehension. When I can't see how, He always makes a way. Even when His way is not my expected way. When I'm faced with a mountain, He moves it. When I face an obstacle, He knocks it down. There are times when it's easier said than to understand. I question, I ask, I fight, I doubt, I can't see what He's doing, but I know in my heart, His plan and purpose will always be what's best for me because He knows what I need. My encouragement is to rest in the fact that even when we don't understand, He has a plan and it's the best plan for us. Find your peace and comfort in the presence of Jesus and believe that He's working, even when we can't see it.

PRAYER

Dear Heavenly Father, my faith, my hope and my trust are in You alone. Work in my heart and help me to walk courageously as the person You've created me to be. I believe You have the answers to all of my questions, and You will reveal them when the time is right. You have my full trust. Thank You Jesus. Amen.

NOTES

MEANING

What does today's scripture mean to you?

_____

_____

_____

_____

_____

_____

_____

_____

_____

APPLICATION

How can you apply this to your day?

_____

_____

_____

_____

_____

_____

_____

_____

_____

DAY FOUR

"Let us not become weary in doing good, for at the proper time we will reap a harvest if we do not give up."

Galatians 6:9

Change doesn't happen overnight. It's a process. Doing something for a week and expecting drastic results is crazy. You have to put in the time, the work and the effort before seeing a change. Unfortunately, consistency is something many people lack. In order to remain consistent, we need to apply small daily efforts, compounded over a period of time and that will get you to where you want to be. For example, if you want to pray more, don't start with a two-hour fasting and prayer, start by setting aside five to ten minutes a day, getting into His presence consistently and increase as you go. Once it becomes second nature and an established practice, try a little longer and more often. Rather than trying to read the Bible for an hour a day, five days a week, right out the gate, start with reading just a page or two every day. Do that consistently for a week or two and as it becomes a habit, add more to your reading schedule. It's small efforts like these that's done over a long period of time that makes good habits solidified and easier to do. It might not seem like enough, but this is how change happens. You can apply this practice to anything in life you want to change.

PRAYER

God, though I may become weak, tired or run down, You alone are my strength. In the middle of the storm my eyes are fixed on You because You are good and faithful. I trust the path You have me on because I know that You will lead and guide me in the direction that will bring You glory and honor. Thank You. In Jesus name, amen.

NOTES

_____

_____

_____

_____

MEANING

What does today's scripture mean to you?

_____

_____

_____

_____

_____

_____

_____

_____

<u>APPLICATION</u>

How can you apply this to your day?

_____

_____

_____

_____

_____

_____

_____

_____

DAY FIVE

"Therefore do not be ashamed of the testimony about our Lord, nor of me his prisoner, but share in suffering for the gospel by the power of God"

2 Timothy 1:8

I have no more shame, guilt, fear, worry, anxiousness, depression or regret. My life is no longer mine. My story has had ups and downs, highs and lows, peaks and valleys. I'm sure you can relate. None of it was in vain. I can say that from the bottom of my heart, Jesus Christ has given me a new outlook on everything that's transpired. Today I am new and it's not by my own doing. Only by His Blood have I been transformed and reborn. And this same gift is available to all who believe. I invite you to walk in the newness that Christ provides.

PRAYER

Lord, I surrender all shame, guilt and regret at the foot of Your throne. I am no longer a slave to my past failures and mistakes, only because the blood of Your Son. You are worthy and deserve honor and praise. Thank You for calling me out of darkness and allowing me to walk in the newness only You provide. In the mighty name of Jesus, amen.

NOTES

_____

_____

_____

_____

MEANING

What does today's scripture mean to you?

_____

_____

_____

_____

_____

_____

_____

_____

APPLICATION

How can you apply this to your day?

_____

_____

_____

_____

_____

_____

_____

_____

DAY SIX

"For you created my inmost being; you knit me together in my mother's womb. I praise you because I am fearfully and wonderfully made; your works are wonderful, I know that full well."

Psalm 139:13-14

Unfortunately, you won't be everybody's favorite cup of tea. Not everyone is going to like you. People will dislike you because of your faith, your looks, your past, your laugh, your style, your personality, and many other things that make you, you! That's alright! Think about this; there were people who didn't like Jesus and He was perfect! In situations where someone is negative towards you or dislikes you, remember who God says you are. Walk in his authority, smile at them and turn the other cheek. What He thinks of you is most important. You are loved, you are worthy, you are a limited edition, one of a kind, hand crafted, exclusive, mold breaking son or daughter of the Most High.

PRAYER

Today I give You praise from my inner most being. I am so filled with gratitude that You thought this world needed me. You know me better than anyone and I'm thankful to have an intimate relationship with the creator of everything. Glory and honor are Yours alone. I pray this all in the name of Jesus Christ. Amen.

NOTES

_____

_____

_____

_____

MEANING

What does today's scripture mean to you?

_____

_____

_____

_____

_____

_____

_____

_____

_____

APPLICATION

How can you apply this to your day?

_____

_____

_____

_____

_____

_____

_____

_____

DAY SEVEN

"We are afflicted in every way, but not crushed; perplexed, but not driven to despair; persecuted, but not forsaken; struck down, but not destroyed."

2 Corinthians 4:8

I just wanted to take a moment to remind you that we are all facing different trials and tribulations. Each and every person reading this has their own issues and obstacles they're fighting. No one is immune to life hardships. But the encouragement, the joy, the beauty of it all is that if you are a believer in Jesus Christ, you have the victory. The power that is in you is greater than the power in this world. At the end of the day, God has the final say. Don't ask God to take away your problems, ask Him to be the strength that gets you through them.

PRAYER

Dear Heavenly Father, I find comfort knowing that I am never alone. You are my fortress, my comfort, my peace and my portion. As I go through the obstacles of life, I'm encouraged knowing that if anything is too great for me, I have You. Thank You Lord. Amen.

NOTES

_____

_____

_____

_____

MEANING

What does today's scripture mean to you?

_____

_____

_____

_____

_____

_____

_____

_____

APPLICATION

How can you apply this to your day?

_____

_____

_____

_____

_____

_____

_____

_____

_____

DAY EIGHT

"You will seek Me and find Me when you search for Me with all your heart."

Jeremiah 29:13

In my past teachings, I have read this verse and it has rubbed some people the wrong way. Here's the thing, personally, I don't want a list of what I can or cannot do. I don't want rituals. What I want is a relationship, love, correction, direction, forgiveness, grace and guidance. I want what the law can never satisfy. I want what only Jesus is able to provide. For years, I've searched for this. Yet it wasn't until I surrendered it all and accepted Jesus Christ as my savior when I found it. If you want to know Him better, pursue Him. If you want His presence, seek it. Nothing fills my cup or quenches my thirst like the real and living Holy Spirit of God. You need to look for Him like you would look for your car keys on the first day of a new job and you're running late. It's urgent.

PRAYER

God in Heaven, it brings me peace knowing that You are always with me. I give You all my cares, worries and fears and I ask for Your divine comfort. I set aside time to seek You. To know You. I ask that You write Your word on my heart. I hold tight to Your promises as I know You are good and faithful to answer. Thank You for all that You do. In Jesus name, amen.

NOTES

_____

_____

_____

_____

MEANING

What does today's scripture mean to you?

_____

_____

_____

_____

_____

_____

_____

_____

APPLICATION

How can you apply this to your day?

_____

_____

_____

_____

_____

_____

_____

_____

DAY NINE

"But seek first his kingdom and his righteousness, and all these things will be given to you as well."

Matthew 6:33

How do you build a better relationship with God? You communicate with Him through prayer, learn about who He is by reading His word, worship Him with all your heart and then repeat. This is easier said than done when you're a parent, going to school, full-time work, being a caretaker, attending commitments or any other duties that fill your week. Which leads me to ask, if you were trying to build a business partner relationship, a personal relationship or parent/child relationship, what would you have to do? You would have to communicate, learn who they are and love them. Building a relationship with God takes the same steps. The harder you pursue Him the closer you get. The closer you get to Him, the clearer His voice becomes. If you want to have a better relationship with God, He has to be first. This is non-negotiable.

PRAYER

Lord God I put You first. I set aside all distractions and put You at the forefront of my thoughts. I am making space in my heart, my mind and my life for You to reign. Anything that keeps me from pursuing You, I lay down at the foot of Your throne. I am Yours. Thank You Jesus, amen.

NOTES

_____

_____

_____

_____

<u>MEANING</u>

What does today's scripture mean to you?

_____

_____

_____

_____

_____

_____

_____

_____

<u>APPLICATION</u>

How can you apply this to your day?

_____

_____

_____

_____

_____

_____

_____

_____

DAY TEN

"Blessed is the man who remains steadfast under trial, for when he has stood the test he will receive the crown of life, which God has promised to those who love him."

James 1:12

We have so much to be grateful for. Life itself is a gift. Regardless of the trials, tribulations, storms, troubles, obstacles and issues we have, God is on the throne. We are blessed to know Him. We should be beyond thankful if we're saved, know Jesus and are filled with the Holy Spirit because regardless of what we experience while on Earth, we can be sure we won't have to deal with God's wrath in the end. Count all your blessings no matter how small or large, and thank God for grace, forgiveness and the blood of Jesus.

PRAYER

Heavenly Father I pray that You would create a steadfast spirit in me. Give me a spirit of discipline and consistency. I want to live a life that is pleasing to You. Teach me Your ways and lead me with Your Holy Spirit. I ask that You take away anything that distances me from Your will and purpose for my life. Amen.

NOTES

_____

_____

_____

_____

<u>MEANING</u>

What does today's scripture mean to you?

_____

_____

_____

_____

_____

_____

_____

_____

APPLICATION

How can you apply this to your day?

_____

_____

_____

_____

_____

_____

_____

_____

_____

DAY ELEVEN

*"Do not conform any longer to the pattern
of this world but be transformed by the
renewing of your mind. Then you will be
able to test and approve what God's will
is—his good, pleasing and perfect will."*

Romans 12:2

For years, I have fought battles with my
fist. Now, the word of God is my sword,
there's power in my prayer and I worship
my maker in the midst of all of the storms. I
no longer try to fit in, please others or
follow the masses. I renew my mind daily
by challenging my thoughts, ideas and
beliefs with the word of God. I make sure
that what I'm doing and how I'm living lines
up with how God calls us to live. This world
is constantly sending us messages of
what's important and how we should spend
our time, but we have to remind ourselves

daily that the worlds wisdom is in direct opposition of Godly wisdom. Make sure that you don't get comfortable following the crowd but that you're using the word of God as your compass. Being a Christian is radical, offensive and against the grain. In a world that tries to normalize and desensitize us to wickedness and sin, we stand out as a light in a very dark and hurting world. Be the light someone needs.

PRAYER

Father God give me a new mind. Take away all desires, thoughts and behaviors that no longer serve me as I pursue the plan You have for my life. I lay down my goals, visions and dreams at the foot of Your throne and ask that You would resurrect me in the image of who You have called me to be. I ask this in the name of Jesus, amen.

NOTES

_____

_____

_____

_____

<u>MEANING</u>

What does today's scripture mean to you?

_____

_____

_____

_____

_____

_____

_____

_____

APPLICATION

How can you apply this to your day?

_____

_____

_____

_____

_____

_____

_____

_____

DAY TWELVE

"Humility is the fear of the LORD; its wages are riches and honor and life."

Proverbs 22:4

The world doesn't revolve around you. There are other people living in it. The world tells us to be selfish and prideful. It teaches us that we're untouchable. It whispers in our ear that we're better than others, entitled, that we have to step on others to get where we want to go. The world brainwashes us with an "above others" concept and makes us feel like we're more important than others. That's wrong! Our confidence and purpose should only come from Christ, the word of God and the promises of the Bible. I've experienced the world and was quickly brought back to humility. It wasn't fun and it wasn't kind. My eyes are now fixed on

Jesus and my boldness, authority and confidence are found in Him. Always remember to remain in a constant state of humility.

PRAYER

God in Heaven, I humbly come into Your presence with a desire to give You praise, honor and worship. I look at the life I have, and although I don't have everything I want, I know that You provide everything I need, and for that I am grateful. Help me to live a life that brings glory to Your name alone. I pray this in the power of Your name, amen.

NOTES

_____

_____

_____

_____

<u>MEANING</u>

What does today's scripture mean to you?

_____

_____

_____

_____

_____

_____

_____

_____

APPLICATION

How can you apply this to your day?

_____

_____

_____

_____

_____

_____

_____

_____

_____

DAY THIRTEEN

"Let not your hearts be troubled. Believe in God; believe also in me."

John 14:1

Belief is having trust, faith, or confidence in someone or something. We should all be confident in our relationship with God because the promises found in the word of God are immutable. We all should have faith that He is who He says He is and trust every aspect of our life in His hands. Fear, anxiety and worry no longer control our life because our hope is in Jesus. Rest easy knowing God will take all your burdens away for you in His perfect timing. If you find yourself struggling with unbelief, look no further than the word of God for comfort and refuge. We have to make it a daily practice to pick up the Bible and search for the promises of God. There's no source of comfort that this world has to offer that can compare to His word. If it's not from God, then it's only a band aid that will eventually fall off and have you searching for another temporary solution.

PRAYER

Father God, I lay all of my troubles down. I believe that whatever I'm facing is a part of Your plan and that You will give me the strength to overcome. Help me see the purpose in the pain. My faith, my hope and my trust are firmly in You. I stand on the promises of Your word and will not be shaken because You are my rock. Thank You lord. In Jesus name, I pray, amen.

NOTES

_____

_____

_____

_____

MEANING

What does today's scripture mean to you?

_____

_____

_____

_____

_____

_____

_____

_____

_____

APPLICATION

How can you apply this to your day?

_____

_____

_____

_____

_____

_____

_____

_____

_____

DAY FOURTEEN

"For all have sinned and fall short of the glory of God..."

Romans 3:23

This is a foundational teaching of the Word of God as we are all guilty of sinning. Sin separates us from God and because none of us are sinless, Jesus paid the price for us to have access to Him. There's no other way to reconcile the relationship except by the blood of Jesus Christ. As we learn this, we need to focus on living a righteous life that honors God. Though we will make mistakes and fall short of the glory of God, knowing salvation is only accessible through Christ should be our daily inspiration to be better and do better.

PRAYER

Lord God without You I am lost. I have sinned against You. I have made mistakes, I have failed and I have fallen short too many times to count. Wash me in the blood of Jesus and help me to turn from anything that pushes me away from You. I draw near in expectation knowing that the Holy Spirit in me is changing me at this moment. I thank You for Your love, mercy and grace. In Jesus name, amen.

NOTES

_____

_____

_____

<u>MEANING</u>

What does today's scripture mean to you?

_____

_____

_____

_____

_____

_____

_____

_____

_____

<u>APPLICATION</u>

How can you apply this to your day?

_____

_____

_____

_____

_____

_____

_____

_____

DAY FIFTEEN

"Trust in the LORD with all your heart and do not lean on your own understanding. In all your ways acknowledge Him, And He will make your paths straight."

Proverbs 3:5-6

God has a plan for each and every one of us. I wish I could always see what He sees or had a better understanding of what He's doing, but it doesn't work that way. Faith is believing and trusting in the unseen and unknown. I believe that His plan for my life far outweighs anything I could plan. This verse reminds me that He is in control and if I just draw near and keep my eyes on Him, everything will work out as it should. Less of me, more of you Lord, I surrender.

PRAYER

Dear Heavenly Father, I know that Your ways are greater than mine. I often think with the limitations of being human. I ask for You to teach me Your ways. Help me to surrender my own plans and purposes for Your will. I submit my way of thinking and ask that You'd give me eyes to see and ears to hear so that my ways bring You glory, honor and praise. I ask in the name of Jesus, amen.

NOTES

_____

_____

_____

<u>MEANING</u>

What does today's scripture mean to you?

_____

_____

_____

_____

_____

_____

_____

_____

_____

<u>APPLICATION</u>

How can you apply this to your day?

_____

_____

_____

_____

_____

_____

_____

_____

DAY SIXTEEN

"Train up a child in the way he should go; even when he is old, he will not depart from it."

Proverbs 22:6

As a father I've failed, I've made mistakes, I've fallen short and I'm sure there'll be more in the future. Raising kids doesn't come with a manual. What I've learned is each kid responds differently to different tactics. Not having a father growing up I've had to piece it all together. I've witnessed many great examples, experienced terrible examples and along the way I take notes and try to be the best version of a father I can be. The one thing that's my go to and never fails me is the word of God. That is where I find my example, my direction and my instruction. Despite my flaws I can count on God and the Holy Spirit to help me raise my children and help them become God fearing men. My recommendation for you is not to be the perfect parent, but to be a parent who's present, willing and able to direct them onto the righteous path God has called us all to follow. If you don't have children of your own, this also applies to children in your friend, family or church communities.

PRAYER

Father in Heaven help me to see the direction You're leading me. I know that You have a plan and purpose for my life, and I want nothing more than to live that out. If the direction I'm going doesn't line up with where You want me to go, I pray that You would redirect and put me back on Your path. I ask this in the name of Jesus Christ, amen.

NOTES

_____

_____

_____

_____

MEANING

What does today's scripture mean to you?

_____

_____

_____

_____

_____

_____

_____

_____

APPLICATION

How can you apply this to your day?

_____

_____

_____

_____

_____

_____

_____

_____

_____

DAY SEVENTEEN

"Casting all your anxieties on him, because he cares for you."

1 Peter 5:7

Worry, fear and anxiety are all from the enemy. Those are tactics to try and make you question God or provoke doubt. News flash! He is in control. At the end of the day there is so much in life that is out of our control. Having faith and surrendering our anxious feelings to God is the only answer. He wants us to come to Him with everything. All of those worries, doubt, fears and things that make us anxious. If you want rest, peace of mind, answers and solutions to your problems, they're all found in an intimate relationship with our Lord and Savior, Jesus Christ.

PRAYER

Lord I know that You haven't given me a spirit of fear, worry or anxiety. I know that any thought like that isn't from You. I ask that You tear down any tactics of the enemy that try to distract me or pull my attention away from You. Thank You for the power of the blood of Your son Jesus. In His name I pray, amen.

NOTES

_____

_____

_____

_____

MEANING

What does today's scripture mean to you?

_____

_____

_____

_____

_____

_____

_____

_____

APPLICATION

How can you apply this to your day?

_____

_____

_____

_____

_____

_____

_____

_____

DAY EIGHTEEN

"Your word is a lamp to my feet and a light to my path."

Psalm 119:105

Life for me doesn't look the same as it did a year ago. That's probably the same for most of you as so much changes in a year. I wouldn't have imagined my life as it is now if you would've told me about it. I would have said you're crazy. Yet here I am. Not the path I chose, not what I'm comfortable doing, not my childhood dream. I will say this, I've never been more fulfilled, had more purpose, a clearer vision or as happy following the plan and purpose God had for me. Truly, God knows best. His plan is the only plan and He doesn't make mistakes. If you're wrestling with what God's plan is for your life, pursue Him, talk to Him about it and ask that He opens the doors to your purpose. The closer you get to Him, the clearer His voice is.

PRAYER

Heavenly Father, I pray that You would reveal Yourself through Your word. Speak to me, teach me and guide me as I look no further than Your word for guidance. I want nothing more than to follow the path You've laid out in front of me, so I ask for You to be my compass. Ignite a Holy fire in my soul that burns for Your Holy presence. I pray this is in the name of Your son Jesus Christ, amen.

NOTES

_____

_____

_____

MEANING

What does today's scripture mean to you?

_____

_____

_____

_____

_____

_____

_____

_____

APPLICATION

How can you apply this to your day?

_____

_____

_____

_____

_____

_____

_____

_____

_____

DAY NINETEEN

"Strengthening the souls of the disciples, encouraging them to continue in the faith, and saying that through many tribulations we must enter the kingdom of God."

Acts 14:22

We all have imperfections, struggles, and issues. No one has it truly figured out. As for me, I'm trying to do the best I can with what God has given me and placing my faith, hope and trust firmly in the hands of the Lord. He knows I've made many mistakes. He knows I've learned from those mistakes and He knows I will continue to make mistakes. With the remainder of my life, I'm laying it all down at the foot of His throne. My life isn't mine, I'm here to serve Him and His people. Be encouraged my friends, we're in this together and God has a plan.

PRAYER

Dear God, I know things that I'm experiencing in life are meant to strengthen me, grow me and refine me into who You've created me to be. Help me to see the purpose in the pain and to hold tight to Your promises. Help me to anchor my soul in Your word. I can only carry so much of this burden. I look to You for help because I know You hear my cry for help. In Jesus name, amen.

NOTES

_____

_____

_____

<u>MEANING</u>

What does today's scripture mean to you?

_____

_____

_____

_____

_____

_____

_____

_____

<u>APPLICATION</u>

How can you apply this to your day?

_____

_____

_____

_____

_____

_____

_____

_____

_____

DAY TWENTY

"My sheep hear my voice, and I know them, and they follow me."

John 10:27

God's will for your life won't always make sense to others and that's okay. It's between you and God. It's your relationship and it's contingent on your faith, your trust, your love, your willingness and your desire to follow Him. Remember, the apostles meant well when as they tried to discourage Jesus from going to the cross, but He knew God's will and they didn't. People can't hear when God whispers in your ear. Sadly, some people can't hear God even when He whispers into their ears. When God speaks to us, it requires a level of intimacy and closeness to Him that some aren't willing to pursue. They allow distractions of this world to over speak Him. My advice is to draw near to God and follow His voice despite what people on the sidelines have to say.

PRAYER

God in Heaven, I pray that You would give me ears to hear Your voice. I long for direction and guidance. I draw near to You knowing that You will draw near to me. I set aside all distractions and anything that takes my eyes away from You. Help me to follow the plan and purpose You have for my life; I want nothing more. In the mighty name of Jesus, I pray, amen.

NOTES

_____

_____

_____

_____

<u>MEANING</u>

What does today's scripture mean to you?

_____

_____

_____

_____

_____

_____

_____

_____

APPLICATION

How can you apply this to your day?

_____

_____

_____

_____

_____

_____

_____

_____

DAY TWENTY-ONE

"And Jesus answered them, "Have faith in God. Truly, I say to you, whoever says to this mountain, 'Be taken up and thrown into the sea,' and does not doubt in his heart, but believes that what he says will come to pass, it will be done for him. Therefore, I tell you, whatever you ask in prayer, believe that you have received it, and it will be yours."

Mark 11:22-24

We all have mountains that need to be moved and obstacles that need to be overcome. Sometimes it's hard to see how we'll defeat them, get around them or battle them. What works for me during these seasons is remembering the God I serve is a God who takes what's impossible for man and makes it possible. We don't always have to understand how, but we should always be confident in knowing who is leading the way. If you're lacking faith, ask God to give you the strength to follow His voice without question and the knowledge to understand His purpose for your life is greater than what you can plan. Trust that even though we don't always see the way, God is in full control. All we have to do is fully surrender to Him.

PRAYER

Father God as I seek You in prayer, I come boldly knowing that the things I ask for in faith that line up with Your will are already mine. I ask that You'd change my heart as I get closer to You. Shape and transform me into who You made me to be. Help me to ask for the things that line up with Your will because I know that what You have for me is better than anything I can dream of. My trust is in You. In the name of Jesus, I pray, amen.

NOTES

_____

_____

_____

<u>MEANING</u>

What does today's scripture mean to you?

_____

_____

_____

_____

_____

_____

_____

_____

APPLICATION

How can you apply this to your day?

_____

_____

_____

_____

_____

_____

_____

_____

DAY TWENTY-TWO

"When I am afraid, I put my trust in you."

Psalm 56:3

Control what you can, accept what you can't and put your trust in God. There are so many things out of our control that worrying about them could be a full-time job. When I feel overwhelmed, nervous, afraid or anxious, I do two things. One, I perform a breath in-and-out technique I found works for me. Two, I sit silently in God's presence reminding myself whose hands are laid on me daily. God's hands! We all experience madness, it just looks different for others compared to yours. It may not make sense and it may not feel fair, but God knows the plan and purpose for the season you are facing. He knows your strengths and weaknesses. That is why our trust has to be in Him and only Him.

PRAYER

*Dear Heavenly Father, I come to praise
You through the fear, depression, worry
and emotions that come from this world.
My trust is firmly in You. Regardless of my
circumstances, You are worthy of my
praise. Here I am to speak of Your glory.
Thank You Lord for being my strong tower
and refuge. Amen.*

NOTES

_____

_____

_____

_____

MEANING

What does today's scripture mean to you?

_____

_____

_____

_____

_____

_____

_____

_____

_____

APPLICATION

How can you apply this to your day?

_____

_____

_____

_____

_____

_____

_____

_____

DAY TWENTY-THREE

*"And be kind to one another,
tenderhearted, forgiving one another, even
as God in Christ forgave you."*

Ephesians 4:32

Life's too short. Death reminds us of that daily. There are many people who pass away with unfinished business, regrets, broken relationships, resentment, unforgiven wrongs and probably a host of other issues. Personally, I don't want that to be me. I want my life to be filled with the fruits of the spirit, love and joy; no regrets or resentment. This is not to say I won't make mistakes or live a perfect life as that's not realistic. Life is filled with "stuff." I can, however, control how I respond and handle things moving forward. Say this declaration with me, "I forgive anything and everything done to me, said to me and said about me. I surrender it all to God. I will no longer carry that in my heart. Each day is a new blank page and I choose to live a life free of baggage. The power to step into this next level of life is found in Christ, so today I claim it and receive it in His mighty name."

PRAYER

Lord I come into Your presence by the blood of Jesus. I ask that You renew my spirit. Search my heart and help me get rid of any thoughts, ideas, feelings or beliefs that don't line up with Your word. Cleanse me of anything that pushes others away and doesn't bring glory to Your name. Help me to love others like Your son Jesus loves the church. I know I can do better. Thank You lord, amen.

NOTES

_____

_____

_____

__MEANING__

What does today's scripture mean to you?

_____

_____

_____

_____

_____

_____

_____

_____

<u>APPLICATION</u>

How can you apply this to your day?

_____

_____

_____

_____

_____

_____

_____

_____

DAY TWENTY-FOUR

"Be still before the Lord and wait patiently for him; fret not yourself over the one who prospers in his way, over the man who carries out evil devices! Refrain from anger and forsake wrath! Fret not yourself; it tends only to evil. For the evildoers shall be cut off, but those who wait for the Lord shall inherit the land."

Psalm 37:7-9

As Christians, it's important for us to be patient and stay in constant prayer with our Father. Whether we see it or not, God's got a plan and it's better than ours. We have to believe it. Don't get caught up with what everyone else is doing or what He's doing in their life. Stay in your lane and keep your eyes focused on Him. The one practice I feel evades many people is the "be still" practice. How many of us actually take the time to be alone with God without any distractions? When I turn off my phone, shut off any music or television playing, get alone and take time to be in God's presence, only then am I able to hear from God. Jesus went off multiple times to be alone with God. Jesus didn't have an iPhone pulling His attention, so if Jesus cut eliminated all distractions, then we should be doing that as well. Unfortunately, for some of us, when we are silent and attempt to be still, our minds fill with thoughts, questions, ideas, worries and a flood of mental noise. It takes time and practice but when those things arise, cancel them out with breathing and bringing your mind back to the presence of God. Over time it gets easier. When you're in a season of waiting and patience, take time to check in with God often and be still.

PRAYER

Father God help me to set aside more time in my life to seek You. I want a better relationship with You, and I know it's up to me to make that happen. I ask for Your assistance in getting rid of any and all distractions. I want to go deeper with You lord. I want to know You better. Help me to be still as I wait patiently for You to move in my life. In the name of Jesus, I pray, amen.

NOTES

_____

_____

_____

_____

MEANING

What does today's scripture mean to you?

_____

_____

_____

_____

_____

_____

_____

_____

APPLICATION

How can you apply this to your day?

_____

_____

_____

_____

_____

_____

_____

_____

DAY TWENTY-FIVE

"But the Lord stood with me and strengthened me, so that the message might be preached fully through me, and that all the Gentiles might hear. Also, I was delivered out of the mouth of the lion."

2 Timothy 4:17

Just a reminder that if you're a Christian, God is with you. He sees you. He hears your prayers. He counts your tears. He loves you. He forgives you. Whatever you're going through, you're not alone. If you're reading this, remember that He's gotten you through all of your previous problems, issues and situations that at one point seemed impossible. Our source of strength comes from the Lord. I hear that God won't give us more than we can handle, but I disagree strongly with that statement. I know that God will give us far more than we can handle in order for us to understand that we can't do it without Him. There will be times in our lives we feel like giving up and can't go any further. If we want to make it, we must tap into His might. He is good and faithful to deliver us from whatever valley we are in, but it's when we stop trying to do it on our own and hold on to the promise that through Him we can do all things.

PRAYER

Heavenly Father I ask that you give me words to speak to the lost. Help me to be a light in this dark world. I want to bring glory to Your name. I offer my life as a living sacrifice and ask that You'd give me opportunities to lead others to a place of repentance and right relationship with You. I ask in faith and pray this in the name Jesus, amen.

NOTES

_____

_____

_____

_____

<u>MEANING</u>

What does today's scripture mean to you?

_____

_____

_____

_____

_____

_____

_____

_____

<u>APPLICATION</u>

How can you apply this to your day?

_____

_____

_____

_____

_____

_____

_____

_____

DAY TWENTY-SIX

"But the LORD said to Samuel, "Do not look at his appearance or at his physical stature, because I have refused him. For the LORD does not see as man sees; for man looks at the outward appearance, but the LORD looks at the heart."

1 Samuel 16:7

"I'm just a nobody, trying to tell everybody, all about somebody, who saved my soul." If you know this saying, then you should know this is exactly how I feel. All I try to do is spread the word of God, pray over people, encourage and help others. Everything I do or say points to our Heavenly Father and Jesus Christ. I give all glory, thanks and praise to God. Without Him I would be dead in my sins. I'm thankful and grateful to be here and don't take that for granted. I wouldn't be where I am today without His favor. The work I do is the work of the kingdom, not of man. If God does not look at my physical appearance, then no man should. We should only focus on the heart of man and what they are doing for the kingdom of God.

PRAYER

God in Heaven, I want to see others as You see them. Help me leave all of my opinions, judgments and faulty beliefs at the foot of Your throne. I want to love others for who they are. I don't want to miss out on Your will, plan or purpose because I get in the way. I humbly ask for eyes to see and a heart of compassion so I can better serve You. I ask this in the name of Jesus, amen.

NOTES

_____

_____

_____

_____

MEANING

What does today's scripture mean to you?

_____

_____

_____

_____

_____

_____

_____

_____

<u>APPLICATION</u>

How can you apply this to your day?

_____

_____

_____

_____

_____

_____

_____

_____

DAY TWENTY-SEVEN

"You also must be patient. Keep your hopes high, for the day of the Lord's coming is near."

James 5:8

They say patience is a virtue. This is one area of my life I've always struggled in. I want what I want, and I want it now. I understand this isn't the right way of thinking and I'm still working on it, one day at a time by the grace of God. What's been helping me in seasons of waiting is resting in His word. When fear, doubt or worry emerge, I battle them with His word. I remind myself of who God is. That He has plans to prosper me. He wants what's best for me. He wants me to be victorious and it's not His plan to withhold anything from me. If I don't have it then it's a message that I don't need it. If His timing is perfect and He doesn't make mistakes, I have to check my ego and pride to make sure that my intentions are pure and the things that I'm praying for are truly from a place to build the kingdom of God, and not my own selfish desires. It's okay to ask and pray for personal desires, goals, dreams and visions, but we have to understand that no is a very real answer to a prayer. If it doesn't line up with what God has for me, I have to humbly accept that. In your season of waiting, being patient is much easier when you are grounded and anchored in His word, constantly praying and doing some self-reflection.

PRAYER

Dear God, I know that Your timing is perfect. I pray that You would calm my nerves, calm my anxieties and help me to be more patient. I want to know in my heart that if it's meant to be then it will happen. I no longer want to rush through life. Help me to enjoy the process and embrace the season of waiting. You alone are God, so my hope will not waver when things don't happen according to my plan. Thank You Lord. Amen.

NOTES

_____

_____

_____

MEANING

What does today's scripture mean to you?

_____

_____

_____

_____

_____

_____

_____

_____

APPLICATION

How can you apply this to your day?

_____

_____

_____

_____

_____

_____

_____

_____

DAY TWENTY-EIGHT

"Let us hold fast the confession of our hope without wavering, for He who promised is faithful."

Hebrews 10:23

Hope is commonly used as a wish for something to happen. Its' strength is the strength of the person's desire. In the Bible, however, hope is the confident expectation of what God has promised and its' strength is in His faithfulness. As Christians, we don't wish. God isn't a genie. He's not here to grant us our wildest dreams. We are His children and He always knows what's best for us. That means that what we want and what we need are completely different things and we have to be aware of that. God is good and faithful and will always provide what we need when it's time. I now understand that an unanswered prayer is a redirection. It can be disappointing and even defeating because we're putting so much energy and effort into trying to make something happen, but God is sovereign. We can't strongarm Him to do what we want and many times that unanswered prayer is Him protecting us. It's not that God isn't hearing us, it's that we have to accept His answer may be no or not right now. God will lead, guide and direct our lives by answering and not answering our prayers. If the answer is no, we have to come back to the place that our unwavering hope comes from His faithful promises. If we fully trust and have faith in God that shouldn't change based on whether we get what we want. He truly knows best and that's where our hope should be.

PRAYER

God, You are good and faithful. There is no one like You. You don't lie, You don't make mistakes and You never leave me. I praise You from the deepest chambers of my heart. Nothing compares to Your love, mercy and grace. Thank You for loving me and allowing me to reconcile myself to You through the blood of Your son Jesus Christ, amen.

NOTES

_____

_____

_____

_____

MEANING

What does today's scripture mean to you?

_____

_____

_____

_____

_____

_____

_____

_____

_____

<u>APPLICATION</u>

How can you apply this to your day?

_____

_____

_____

_____

_____

_____

_____

_____

DAY TWENTY-NINE

"May the God of hope fill you with all joy and peace as you trust in him, so that you may overflow with hope by the power of the Holy Spirit."

Romans 15:13

My hope isn't in this life. My worth isn't determined by this world. My source of peace and joy doesn't come from material things. I've tasted and experienced what the world had to offer, and I was left hungry for more. Only in Christ did I found purpose, vision, direction and true joy. Everything else has been a distraction. True joy and genuine happiness start with salvation through the blood of Jesus Christ. If you're saved, that's a pretty good reason to smile today. Being filled with joy, peace and hope is an inside job. The enemy will come to steal your happiness with thoughts of shame, regret, guilt and fear. It's up to us to stand on the word of God to battle back. We must remind ourselves of who we are according to God. Our identity, our worth and our purpose is all found within. How do we know if we don't read God's word? Lean on the power of the Holy Spirit to bring to memory any verses we can stand on when under attack.

PRAYER

Father in Heaven I pray that You would fill me so I'm overflowing with Your Holy Spirit. I know that true happiness and joy are found only in You. I reject anything that tells me otherwise. The things of this world pale in comparison to a right relationship with You. Lead me with Your Holy Spirit down the path of righteousness and help me live a life that brings honor to Your name. In Jesus name, amen.

NOTES

_____

_____

_____

MEANING

What does today's scripture mean to you?

_____

_____

_____

_____

_____

_____

_____

_____

_____

APPLICATION

How can you apply this to your day?

_____

_____

_____

_____

_____

_____

_____

_____

DAY THIRTY

"Happy are the people whose God is the Lord."

Psalm 144:15

This life is a vapor. Here today, gone tomorrow. We all have trials, tribulations, struggles, obstacles and issues. They just vary by degree. You're not alone. Despite not being where you want or facing a storm, it's up to us to make the most of our time here. Happiness is a choice. If you're saved, know Jesus and are breathing, that should be enough to make you smile. If all you have is Jesus, then you have all you need. At the end of the day our portion is in Heaven, not here on Earth. Take a minute to reflect on the glory of God and tell Him thank you, despite your situation. Be encouraged by the fact that not everyone has been chosen and set aside to receive the divine revelation that Jesus Christ is the Son of God. When life has you down and the enemy is trying to still your joy, find a position of praise despite what we're going through in life. Our circumstances don't change the character of God and He is worthy to be praised.

PRAYER

Father God, I am so thankful that You chose me, that You hand crafted me and that You designed me in my mothers' womb. I will praise You all the days of my life. I'm honored and humbled that You would share the divine revelation of Your Son Jesus Christ. I ask that You direct my steps according to Your purpose so that I can experience the fullness of walking in complete obedience to You. Thank You Lord. Amen.

NOTES

_____

_____

_____

<u>MEANING</u>

What does today's scripture mean to you?

_____

_____

_____

_____

_____

_____

_____

_____

APPLICATION

How can you apply this to your day?

_____

_____

_____

_____

_____

_____

_____

_____

DAY THIRTY-ONE

"You are of God, little children, and have overcome them, because He who is in you is greater than he who is in the world."

1 John 4:4

Every single day we have to get up and seek God. Our flesh and spirit are constantly at war with one another. We have to die daily and pick up our cross. Being a Christian isn't always a walk in the park. There is constant distraction, fighting for your attention and trying to take your focus off God. We have to remember that He who is in us, is greater than he who is this world. Don't forget who you are! We are children of God. It was done and fully completed when Jesus died on the cross and was resurrected. We have power and authority over this world. As children of the Most High, we must walk boldly and courageously. Remind yourself this anytime you start to get weary or are under attack. Tap in daily through prayer, reading your word, equipping your armor and seeking His Holy presence.

PRAYER

Dear Heavenly Father, I boldly come before Your throne only by the blood of Your Son Jesus. Teach me Your ways. Write Your word on my heart. Help me live a life that inspires, encourages and changes people's lives. I want every choice, decision and action to line up with Your will so my life will bring glory to You alone. I love You, I thank You and I praise You. In Jesus mighty name I pray, amen.

NOTES

_____

_____

_____

MEANING

What does today's scripture mean to you?

_____

_____

_____

_____

_____

_____

_____

_____

_____

<u>APPLICATION</u>

How can you apply this to your day?

_____

_____

_____

_____

_____

_____

_____

_____

_____

Made in the USA
Columbia, SC
07 March 2021